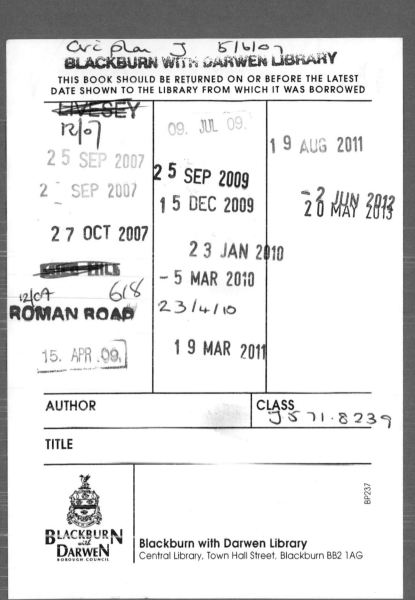

Looking at Lifecycles

Daisy

Victoria Huseby

FRANKLIN WATTS
LONDON•SYDNEY

First published in 2007 by Franklin Watts
338 Euston Road, London NW1 3BH

Franklin Watts Australia
Level 17/207 Kent Street
Sydney NSW 2000

Editor: Rachel Tonkin
Designer: Proof Books
Picture researcher: Diana Morris
Science consultant: Andrew Solway
Literacy consultant: Gill Matthews
Illustrations: John Alston

Picture credits:
Niall Benvie/OSF: 11; John Crellin/Photographers Direct: 17b, 21; Holt Studios/FLPA Images: 7, 19;
Sally Morgan/Ecoscene: 9; Opla/Shutterstock: 15; Photogenes: 4; Emilia Stasiak/Shutterstock: 13;
Emma Tumman/Photographers Direct: front cover; Craig Tuttle/Corbis: 1, 5

Every attempt has been made to clear copyright.
Should there be any inadvertent omission please
apply to the publisher for rectification.

A CIP catalogue record for this book
is available from the British Library
ISBN: 978 0 7496 7109 9

Dewey Classification: 583'.99

Printed in Malaysia

Franklin Watts is a division of Hachette Children's Books.

Contents

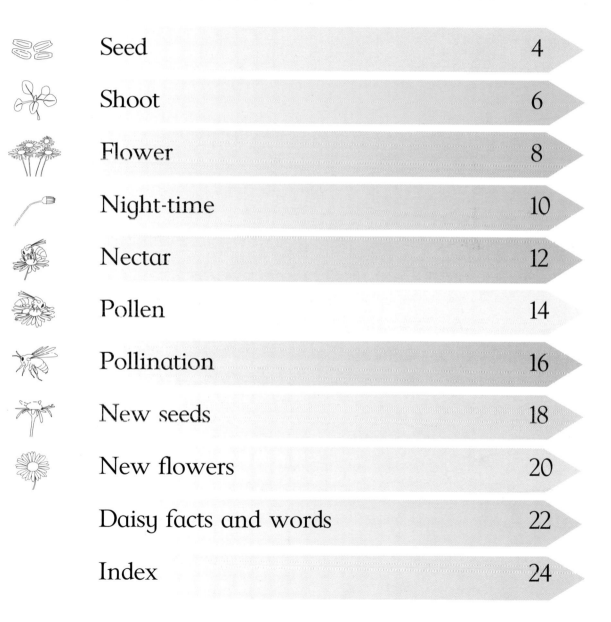

Seed

A daisy is a plant with **flowers** that grows in fields and gardens. It grows from a tiny **seed**.

Daisy seeds

(actual size three millimetres)

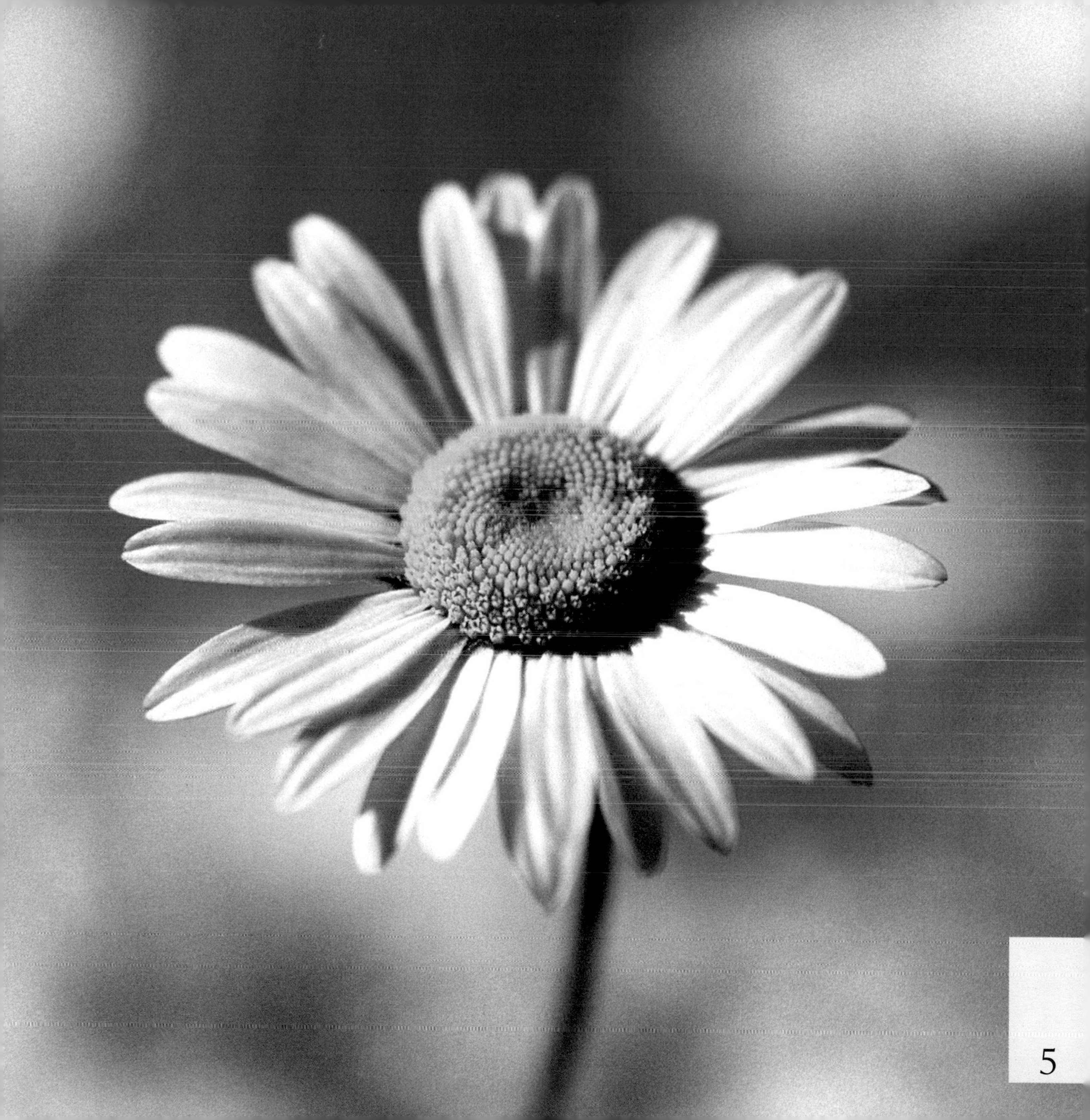

Shoot

In the Spring, the seed begins to grow in the **soil**. A **shoot** grows up out of the seed. Leaves grow from the shoot.

7

Flower

When the daisy is one or two weeks old, it grows a flower. The flower has white **petals** and a yellow **flower head** at its centre.

Night-time

At night, when it is dark,
the daisy's flower closes up.
In the morning, when it
is light, the flower opens
up again.

11

Nectar

During the day, **insects** visit the daisy's flower to drink the sweet **nectar** that it makes.

Pollen

As the insect drinks the nectar, yellow **pollen** from the daisy sticks to it. The insect then flies off to visit another daisy.

15

Pollination

The insect moves the pollen on from the first daisy to the new daisy. The new daisy is now **pollinated**. It can grow seeds.

New seeds

After the daisy has been
pollinated, its petals drop off.
Seeds form in the yellow
flower head.

New flowers

Some seeds fall to the ground. Others are blown away in the wind or carried away by animals. The seeds lie in the soil all Winter. In the Spring, new daisies grow.

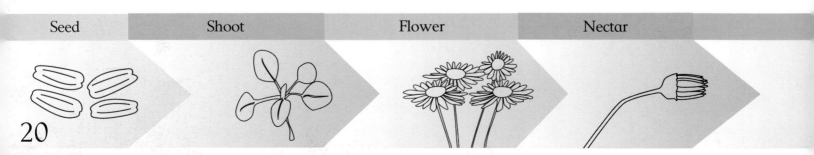

Seed · Shoot · Flower · Nectar

Pollen	Pollination	New seeds	New flowers

21

Daisy facts

• The name daisy probably comes from 'day's eye', because the daisy's flower opens during the day and closes at night.

• Plants are given scientific names in Latin. The Latin name for a daisy is 'Bellis'. It means pretty.

• Daisies used to be used as medicine. They were called 'bruisewort', because they were believed to be good for healing bruises.

• Daisies come from the biggest family of flowering plants in the world. There are around 20,000 different kinds of daisy.

Daisy words

flower
The colourful parts of a plant.

flower head
The middle part of the flower where seeds form.

insects
Animals with six legs and two antennae, or feelers.

nectar
Sweet liquid found in flowers.

petals
The outer parts of a flower.

pollen
A powder found in the flowers of plants. Pollen must be moved from one plant to another for new seeds to form.

pollinated
When a flower can grow new seeds.

seed
The part of a plant that grows to make a new plant.

shoot
The first growth of a young plant above the ground. Shoot also means any new growth, such as a bud or branch, from a plant.

soil
The earth that plants grow in.

Index